THE SILENCE BETWEEN WORDS

CONTENTS

To the silence that twists the mind,
And to those who crave what it hides.

Devotion

The journey begins in the *Veils of the Self*, where we hide behind layers—both conscious and unconscious—that distort who we truly are. We become masters of wearing masks, protecting ourselves not only from the world but from the very essence of our being. Beneath the surface, something stirs, a quiet pull that whispers we cannot remain hidden forever. We stand at the edge of a truth we've long avoided, and though the fall into uncertainty waits, we feel ourselves being pulled into it, powerless to stop what's coming.

Suddenly, we are thrust *Into the Tempest*, where everything we thought we knew is violently shattered. The calm we held onto slips away, and chaos takes its place. It's not just uncomfortable; it's a storm that strips us bare, forcing us to face the raw, unspoken truths we've long avoided. But as the storm rages, we start to unravel, and the stories we've told ourselves fall apart. It's here, in the chaos, that we are forced to confront our deepest fears.

Through the *Fires of Revelation*, we are forged in the flames of transformation. What burns away isn't easy to lose, but it clears the path for something truer, something more real. In this crucible, we discover the true cost of growth: old versions of ourselves must die so that the new can rise. And though the heat is unbearable, we find clarity amid the ashes. We emerge from the flames, scarred, but deeply connected to who we truly are.

In the stillness, we encounter the *Echoes of the Unspoken*, where silence speaks louder than words ever could. The truth lingers in the spaces between, waiting, heavy with the things left unsaid. It's a truth so dense, so impossible to voice. Yet, in the quiet, we begin to hear it—the whispers that tell us who we were always meant to be, the whispers we've been too afraid to hear.

Freedom calls, but it comes with a price. In the **Chains and Choices** we face, the weight of what binds us is more suffocating than we ever realized. These chains are often invisible—formed by fears, past mistakes, and self-imposed limitations—but they are real. Breaking free is not simple, not easy. And yet, we must choose. We must decide whether to stay shackled or unearth the power to shape the life we've been yearning for.

The Path of Power is not about control—it is the quiet reclamation of our own strength. True power isn't loud or forceful; it is found in the decisions we make, in the trust we place in our instincts, and in the courage to move forward without looking back. The real power lies in the unspoken moments, when we stand tall in our truth, unshaken by the echoes of the past.

At **Reflections at the Crossroads**, we are confronted with moments that demand choice. The weight of these decisions presses down on us, but in that pressure, we realize something: the power to choose is ours. The road ahead may feel uncertain, but we've learned that our inner sense of direction is the most reliable guide. It is often in those moments of doubt, when we feel most lost, that our path forward becomes clearer.

The **Journey of Becoming** unfolds not as a destination, but as an evolution. Each step shapes us, each struggle takes us closer to who we are meant to be. Becoming is never about arrival—it is about constant transformation, the courage to evolve, and the willingness to embrace the unknown. The road may stretch on, but the power lies in the journey itself—in the choice to keep going, to continue evolving, and to trust the mystery of who we are becoming.

Targeted Audience

This collection speaks to those on a journey of deep self reflection, growth, and healing.

Those Seeking Clarity
Navigating the complexities of life, identity, and emotional change.

Lovers of Thoughtful Expression
Drawn to language that is layered, metaphorical, and introspective.

The Spiritually Curious
Seeking deeper understanding of self and the world, beyond what is visible.

Those Who Embrace Vulnerability
Attracted to honest emotional expression and the raw truth of human experience.

Those Facing Inner Struggles
Looking for comfort and insight through art that speaks to the heart.

Those Challenging the Status Quo
Reflecting on societal expectations and striving for authentic self-expression.

This collection offers a quiet yet powerful space for transformation, guiding readers through the complexities of the human journey.

VEILS OF THE SELF

---

*Exploring the layers of identity, perception, and the quiet battle
between who we are and who we show the world.*

This section invites you to peel back the masks we wear—unraveling
the complexities of self-perception, the silent struggles, and the
truths hidden beneath the surface. In these poems, the journey
towards self-awareness is both chaotic and beautiful, as we confront
our inner shadows and the veils that obscure our truest selves.

A FADED REALITY

Reality slips through my trembling hands,
Fraying like threads in forgotten strands.
The mask you wear drives me insane,
Tearing apart what little remains.

Is there anyone who hears my cry?
I'm drowning beneath this concrete sky,
Struggling to breathe, lost in the haze,
Choking on smoke, caught in a daze.

The heat bears down, a relentless fire—
I hoped life would lift me and take me higher.
Yet here it stands, a wall of despair,
A barrier that chokes the breath of air

The wind howls, threatening to tear me down,
Though I wear a smile, I only drown.
The drivers rush by, blind to the storm,
Unaware of the wreckage I've become, torn.

Before me stretches a path of ruin,
A future unknown, a fate inhuman.
I yearn to break free, to cast off the chains,
But these shackles hold tight, binding my veins.

I raise my voice, but they cannot hear,
Lost in their chaos, consumed by fear.
They turn away, too numb to see,
Oblivious to the lies that smother me.

ECHOES OF THE UNSEEN

In the heart of chaos, as she came to life,
A storm of emotions cut through like a knife.
Lost, terrified, and shattered inside,
Trust felt distant, no place to hide.

Her instincts betrayed her, nothing felt true,
In the depths of her soul, the world's cruel hue.
She ventured deep into the unknown,
Where silent whispers chilled her to the bone.

Shadows danced in the woods so dark,
Offering solace, a fleeting spark,
From the endless ache of being unseen,
In a world where nothing feels serene.

THE BEAUTIFUL CHAOS OF ME

My scars linger in shadows, hidden from view,
Yet I wear a smile, fragile but true.
They cannot fathom the weight that I bear,
The ache of not belonging is lost in the air.

A stranger I am in my skin,
My moods shift like winds, pulling me in.
A whirlwind of thoughts, emotions untamed,
Each day is a tempest, no two are the same.

Who will I become, lost in this strife,
In the beautiful chaos that is my life?

ABYSS OF THE UNSEEN BATTLE

What's the point of chasing what's right,
When every good intention fades from sight?
I reach, unyielding, for the light,
While angels stand, defying the night.

Yet darkness pulls me deeper still,
Demons feast on my aching will.
Reveling in sorrow, they surround my soul,
A shroud of anguish, bearing its toll.

I'm tired of battling this endless tide,
Take my hand and let the darkness be our guide.

REFLECTIONS OF A SHADOW

Oh, Mirror, Mirror on the wall,
Please, I beg you, don't shatter and fall.

My vision is a haze, lost in despair,
Help me uncover the truth lurking there.
Who is this shadow that I see gazing back?
A stranger in my skin, unraveling the track.
I am drowning in confusion, adrift in this sea,
Desperate to discover who I'm truly meant to be.

Who am I? I cry, yearning for a sign.
I peer into the depths, and what greets my eyes?
A soul hollow and aching, a canvas void of light,
An endless abyss staring, and I tremble in fright,
Witnessing my struggle against this relentless fight.

Life has twisted into a riddle so grim,
I'm lost in this world, on the brink, at the rim.
Every moment I seek, I reach for the door,
Dreaming to step into a realm where I can soar.
To embrace a sanctuary filled with pure bliss,
To finally grasp the meaning of our fragile existence.

THE MASQUERADE OF SELF

Clueless
      I plunge into the depths of my soul,
      Unearthing fragments that make me whole,
Yearning to understand this beautiful enigma—
The mystery of my very existence.

A haunting puzzle, a thread unspooled,
I wander like a detective, lost and ruled.
Chasing whispers that vanish in the air,
Led by a stranger's steps, faint and rare.

The more I search, the further I drift,
Caught in a cycle, endlessly adrift.

Lost in the age-old question: Who am I?

I dig for answers, seeking the spark
That ignites joy and lights the dark.

Yet the reflection staring back at me
Feels like a mask, an illusion, a plea—
Hiding the truth of who I'm meant to be.

THE DANCE OF BEING

Being is believing,
a sacred dance where the soul's yearning meets the light.
It's the art of seeing beyond the veil,
yet when the brilliance of truth overwhelms me,
it can fracture the clarity of my sight.

With courage as my compass, I step into the unknown,
embracing the wild and woven fabric of my existence.
As I plunge deeper into the core of my being,
I confront the shadows that whisper from within—
and in this confrontation,
I unearth the path to my liberation.

BENEATH THE MASKS

Everywhere I turn, souls wear their disguise,
Carrying burdens beneath hollowed skies.
The notion we're born pure, with light that gleams,
Feels like a myth, unraveling at the seams.

I sense their motives, the truths they distort,
Craving chaos, hearts fractured, torn apart.
Our minds are clouded, drifting through the night,
And if these thoughts plague me, they echo your sight.

THE DANCE OF BALANCE

In life's fleeting rhythm,
A balance must be found.
Between dusk and dawn,
Where true strength is unbound.

Caught within the tempest of raw sensation
And reason's quiet, steady foundation,
Excess of either leads to a place
Where certainty dissolves without a trace.

A chasm vast between folly and insight's gleam,
In this fragile realm, Truth lets out a muted scream.
In the equilibrium of grace and despair,
Where light and shadow intertwine in the air.

The pulse of bliss and anguish's clasp
Releases the boundless power we grasp.
In the narrow breach of right and wrong,
Rises the force that makes us fierce and strong.

It is the collision of virtue and vice
That sparks the flame, awakening the night.

BEYOND THE VEIL OF REASON

———————————

Madness... A magic so divine,
This life is a stage where shadows shine.
Our souls, eternal, never fade,
Let's break from reason, unafraid.
Let us yearn for what is strange,
And seek the truths beyond our range.

Reflection Prompts

1. A Faded Reality

When have you felt disconnected from reality, and how did you cope with that feeling?

2. Echoes of the Unseen

How has feeling invisible shaped your sense of self, and what could help you feel seen?

3. The Beautiful Chaos of Me

How do you navigate the contradictions within yourself and find peace amidst them?

4. Abyss of the Unseen Battle

What personal struggle taught you resilience, and how did you overcome it?

5. Reflections of a Shadow

When you look at yourself, what parts of you feel unfamiliar or hidden?

Reflection Prompts

6. The Masquerade of Self

What mask are you hiding behind, and how can you begin to remove it?

7. The Dance of Being

How do you balance light and darkness within yourself, and what helps you grow through it?

8. Beneath the Masks

What mask do you wear to protect yourself, and how does it limit you?

9. The Dance of Balance

How do you find harmony between the contrasting forces in your life?

10. Beyond the Veil of Reason

Think of a moment when something beyond logic changed your perspective—how did it affect you?

CHAPTER

II

INTO THE TEMPEST

Confronting the turbulence of the mind, the shadowy forces that shape our emotions, and the storms we must weather within.

This section takes you into the heart of inner chaos, where the light is often denied, and the shadows loom large. Through these poems, you will journey through the tempest of self-doubt, internal battles, and the quiet, yet powerful, forces of fate. As you face the storms of the soul, there is both destruction and transformation—an inevitable reckoning with the fires that burn within and the path to finding peace amidst the storm.

THE LIGHT WE DENY

Everyone believes in the light we seek,
But if they looked within, they'd see we're far from sleek.
A darkness lurks inside, hidden from sight,
Now's the time we confront it, and bring it to light.

Some are taught to care about the judgment they face,
So they craft false versions, hiding in disgrace.
I don't want us to pretend or conform,
I want us to rise and break free from the norm.

Let's transcend the masks we wear,
And stir a storm that shakes the air.
For when we're trapped within our mind,
It's then that we truly start to die, confined.

SHADOWS AND SPARKS

Once you craft the perfect mask to wear,
They'll turn on you when you're not what they expect them
Heaven forbid we ever fall from grace,
For if we do, hate will quicken its chase.

Everyone acts so polished, so prim,
But when you don't, you're the one on a whim.
I want to show you what's truly real—
It starts with acknowledging how we feel.

Humans are flawed, not perfect, you see,
All of us carrying our own debris.
Our fears rise up when the night falls,
For without shadows, there are no light calls.

We all need the right tools to fight,
Be open, be true, and let go of the fright.
Learn from your scars, and heal in time,
Self-love is the key to undoing the climb.

Do what's best for your heart, be true,
But also see the world from another's view.
When a friend falls into the dark,
Don't tear them down—help them find their spark.

THE SHADOW WITHIN

Something stirs inside of me,
She's dark, yet thrilling, wild, and free.
A side of me that won't obey,
Always hidden, locked away.

I lost myself along the way,
Fell victim to a friend's dismay.
Pushed loved ones far, and then, you see,
She emerged and came to me.

Her power was fierce, so I asked her to stay,
And in her grasp, I drifted away.
When weakness crept, I let her lead,
She showed me strength, gave me what I'd need.

But in her shadow, I lost my light,
Kept her close through endless night.
Now there's a battle, a constant fight,
To do what's right, to find the light.

Sharing control, she still holds the key,
But now I'm reclaiming what's left of me.

THE DOOR OF DARKNESS

Death is knocking on your door,
Should you answer, or ignore?
Are you tired of the guilt you feel,
Wondering now if death is real?

Have you ever sat with the dark inside,
And truly listened, not trying to hide?
Taking your time, letting it unwind—
Now judge the secrets that you find.

Will it hurt, or will you survive?
What does it feel like to be alive,
When death stands close as if to say,
"How does it feel to fade away?"

ECHOES OF A SILENT SOUL

Can you truly see me,
Beyond the surface, where my essence dwells?
Do you glimpse the darkness and the light entwined,
The fragile heart that beats in silent spells?

Can you hear me,
In the quiet where my voice is but a whisper?
I ache for words that rise from the deep,
To stir the stillness, to make the silence shiver.

Do you love me?
My heart trembles, a flame so soft, so wild,
Yearning for the warmth your love might bring,
A need that burns like hunger in a child.

Why can't you see me?
Must I shatter all my walls to be revealed?
Expose the truth I guard in secret grief,
For you to touch the wound that I conceal?

Why can't you hear me?
Must I cry aloud until the night is broken?
My tears like thunder, my soul undone,
A desperate plea in every word unspoken.

Why don't you love me?
Can't you feel the storm that rages there?
A tempest wrought in silence, deep within,
Tearing at the edges of my fractured air.

ANCHORED IN THE TEMPEST

Can you be my guiding star,
Through this storm that tears apart?
I'm lost in battle, bruised and worn,
A warrior's heart, but battered, torn.

Stand with me when I'm broken,
So I can heal, my soul unspoken.
Light the path where shadows crawl,
Guide me through this endless fall.

Give me strength to rise again,
Help me see beyond the pain.
Don't just watch as I descend,
Take my hand, be my end.

TEMPEST OF THE HEART

She danced beneath the weeping sky,
Her heart a symphony, soaring high.
Each step, a song of joy unbound,
Yet shadows of sorrow crept around.

He felt the pulse within her chest,
But watched her spirit slowly rest.
Her tears, like raindrops, kissed the earth,
Each one a tale of silent hurt.

But in the depths, betrayal churned,
A storm within her heart returned.
Her eyes, like lightning, split the night,
A hurricane roared, fierce with might.

As tempests raged and winds did howl,
Her silence roared, a primal growl.
Though chaos soared and voices clashed,
Her unspoken truth, a thunderous flash.

FIRES OF FATE

Our demons waltz beneath the moon's pale light,
Twisting in fire's embrace, wild in flight.
I fell into the madness that was you—
A love so fierce, I never thought it true.

Unaware, I tumbled, lost in your grip,
Caught in the tempest, swallowed by the rift.
I was consumed, infatuated by each scar,
Drawn to the beauty hidden beneath the mar.

I gazed at you, with awe and grace,
A storm of pain and beauty etched on your face.
I imagined a life our bodies might weave,
As fate itself whispered, "You must believe."

Reflection Prompts

11. The Light We Deny

What parts of yourself do you hide, and how might confronting them help you embrace your true potential?

12. Shadows and Sparks

What did wearing a mask teach you about yourself, and how can you embrace your flaws to heal and grow?

13. The Shadow Within

What hidden fears or impulses shape your actions, and how can you reclaim your light?

14. The Door of Darkness

What would it feel like to sit with your darkest emotions and confront them directly?

Reflection Prompts

---

15. *Echoes of a Silent Soul*

When have you felt unseen, and how can you express your true self and give yourself the love you need?

---

16. *Anchored in the Tempest*

What or who anchors you during turmoil, and how can you strengthen that anchor for the future?

---

17. *Tempest of the Heart*

What triggers your emotional storms, and how can you honor those emotions in a healthy way?

---

18. *Fires of Fate*

How have intense relationships or experiences shaped your life, and how do you navigate the beauty and destruction they bring?

FIRES OF REVELATION

Exploring the intensity of self-awareness, the unraveling of hidden truths, and the transformative power of confronting what lies beneath the surface.

In this section, the poems ignite the flames of inner revelation, where silence is shattered, and long-buried truths are unearthed. The journey through these words is both a battleground and a rebirth, as you face the raw, often painful revelations that shape your understanding of the self. Through the fires of conflict and the heat of introspection, there is the possibility of profound transformation—an awakening to the truths that were once concealed.

THE ALLURE OF THE UNSEEN

As I peer into the depths of your gaze,
A chilling truth lingers, a silent blaze.
I feel the weight of your twisted games,
Whispers of loss, unspoken names.

No refuge from the guilt that binds,
I'm drawn to shadows where darkness finds.
In the hollow corners of your soul, I tread,
Where secrets stir and call me dead.

You twist the truth with your soft disguise,
While hidden pain dances in your eyes.
The weight of sorrow you refuse to show,
Is the blood that feeds the storm below.

A suffocating pull, a battle untold,
I'm lost in the lies that you've sold.
Yet still, I crave the truth you hide,
Like a moth to the flame, unable to decide.

No escape from the shadows that cling,
No solace where the darkness sings.
But in your silence, I am drawn—
In the void between dusk and dawn.

THE BATTLEGROUND WITHIN

E very emotion that sweeps through me,
I meet it head-on, untamed, and free.
With each fleeting glimpse of this world,
I feel its pulse, mysteries unfurled.

A battlefield within my mind,
Where light and darkness are intertwined.
My thoughts collide in a constant storm,
Where every feeling reshapes and reforms.

I crave the chaos, the fire, the fight—
Am I captive to shadow or the glow of light?
Tethered to the night that calls me near,
Or a warrior rising, shaking off the fear?

Pain, like ink, is carved so deep,
Yet I hold it close, where it silently sleeps.
I journey through its darkened maze,
With quiet strength, in a daze.

In the silence of turmoil, I find my place,
A dance of resilience, between loss and grace.

UNMASKING THE TRUTH

In the recesses of a fractured mind,
We wear our masks, pretending we're fine.
Behind closed eyes, a world unfolds—
Where truth is buried, and silence holds.

The mind plays tricks, a wicked game,
Where logic bends and we're never the same.
We search for answers, yet never find—
For the questions linger, deep in the mind.

We hide in plain sight, afraid to be seen,
In the shadows of thoughts, where we've always been.
The walls we build are crumbling fast,
As we confront the ghosts of our past.

Truth is a mirror, shattered and cracked,
Reflecting all that we've lacked.
We long to heal, yet fear the pain—
For to face the truth is to break the chain.

In the silence, the mind speaks loud,
Whispering lies beneath a shroud.
But beneath the noise, the truth persists,
A jagged edge, wrapped in mist.

We seek the cure, but it lies within,
In the labyrinth of our own skin.
To unmask the self is to lose control,
To face the chaos lurking in the soul.

No more masks, no more pretense,
Only the mind's raw consequence.
In the darkness, we come undone,
And find that truth is never won.

BENEATH THE SILENCE

I am a vessel, filled with broken thought,
A storm that churns in silence, chaos fought.
In the stillness of my mind, shadows speak,
A battle waged inside, the war I seek.

The turbulence within, I cannot ignore,
It claws, it pulls, as I shut every door.
I refuse to be consumed by what I feel,
But in every storm, I lose what's real.

I tremble beneath the weight of truth's demand,
Fingers gripped tight to the shifting sand.
What anchors me, what keeps me whole,
Are fleeting moments of a fractured soul.

I yearn to tear my heart from my chest,
To see the rawness, to test its rest.
But would I remain if I lose what's mine?
A fractured self or something divine?

The path of darkness, a tempting song,
A life of bitterness, a place to belong.
Yet, I refuse to be her—numb and cold,
I won't surrender to the lies I've been told.

I ache to scream, to tear it all apart,
To rip out my heart and make it art.
But even as I break, I'll hold it tight,
For in my destruction, I find my light.

THE FIRE WITHIN

We surrender to fate's quiet pull,
In that fleeting moment, timeless and full.
When your eyes meet mine, a spark ignites,
A fire that dances, both fierce and light.

It binds us in ways we cannot explain,
A force that burns, a quiet strain.
Beneath this fire, truths are unearthed,
Whispered confessions, revealing our worth.

A rebirth emerges from this flame,
A transformation that knows no name.
We are reshaped, our souls entwined,
Yet within, a quiet fear still confined.

A story begins, stretching through time,
An echo of a tale, sublime.
Yet, in the quiet of this connection's reach,
We wonder—can we trust what our hearts preach?

Eternal as it seems, this love we claim,
We question if it's more than just a name.
For in the spark, we find both light and dark,
A journey of the mind, ignited by a single mark.

TAPESTRIES OF THE MIND

In the depths of my mind, I weave fragile tales,
Replaying every word, tracing every trail.
I search for the perfect thread to mend my fractured self,
Hoping the stories I spin will restore my fragile health.

Am I just a dreamer, chasing a fleeting light,
Crafting realities, sculpting my endless night?
I analyze your every glance, every word you say,
Yearning to unlock the mystery that slips away.

But is this madness that holds me in its grip,
Where do I control the visions that my mind slips?
The stories I weave become truths I believe,
My thoughts dictate my emotions,
what I feel, and what I grieve.

A battle rages within, a tug of war I can't escape,
Ensnared in fantasies, caught in their shape.
I live in a world both intoxicating and unreal,
Where the line between dream and truth is hard to feel.

Whether we are in control of our thoughts,
or being controlled by them,
I find myself lost,
unable to distinguish where I end and they begin.

The mind is a maze, a force that we cannot tame,
And in this tangled web, we all play the same game.

Reflection Prompts

19. The Allure of the Unseen

What draws you to people who hide parts of themselves, and what does it reveal about what you might be avoiding or seeking in your own life?

20. The Battleground Within

When you're torn between conflicting emotions, how do you find a way to reconcile these feelings and move forward?

21. Unmasking the Truth

What happens when you reveal something true about yourself that you've been hiding—how does it shift your sense of self?

22. Beneath the Silence

What holds you back from expressing your anger or frustration, and how could releasing these emotions in a healthy way benefit you?

23. The Fire Within

How do you recognize the difference between a connection that feels destined and one that simply arises from circumstance, and what does that mean for your relationships?

24. Tapestries of the Mind

How do the stories you tell yourself about who you are shape the choices you make, and what would happen if you rewrote those stories?

ECHOES OF THE UNSPOKEN

Traversing the quiet spaces where thought becomes imprisonment, where silence speaks louder than words, and where the search for meaning stirs in the depths of the soul.

This section invites you to delve into the unspoken—those moments where words fail, and the mind holds us captive in its labyrinth of contradictions. These poems echo the quiet struggles within, the internal battles fought in silence, and the yearning for light amidst darkness. The search for clarity and truth is tangled with despair, but within that quiet, there is also the potential for understanding, healing, and eventual release from the cages we build for ourselves.

IN THE CAGE OF THOUGHT

Some days, it feels as though my soul is laid bare,
An eerie whisper, a hollow presence in the air.
I ache for solitude,
Crushed in this cage, bound in a stillness that eludes.
My thoughts, like serpents, coil and unwind,
Does he burn for me, or wish to leave me behind?

I hunger for escape,
To slip into the shadows, where my heart might reshape.
But as I drift away from the ones I believed were true,
I wonder—do they care,
or is it all just a mask to see through?

I'm trapped in this torment, my mind's cruel snare,
So I pour my soul on these pages,
searching for solace in despair.

IN THE QUIET BETWEEN DREAMS

You are the final whisper in my thoughts,
The last echo before I surrender to sleep's soft embrace.
As I drift into dreams, it's in that sacred space
where our souls meet once more, entwined and lost.

Your gaze, a flame that kindles desire,
Your touch, a spark that sets my soul afire.
In this breathtaking reverie, love is reborn,
Each moment a bloom, each kiss a new dawn.

You pull me close, your arms a haven of peace,
Your words are a soft melody, urging my fight to never cease.
And when the dawn breaks, it's light painting the skies,
It's you who stirs my soul, igniting the fire in my eyes.

CROWN OF CONTRADICTIONS

When I think of you,
My heart gallops, untamed and wild—
A storm of emotions,
A tempest fierce and beguiled.

Love and bitterness collide,
A chaotic dance within my soul,
Words fall short of naming this fire,
As it blurs the lines and takes control.

You flipped my world with a single glance,
Yet placed a crown upon my brow.
I longed to rise, to touch the sky—
But found myself sinking beneath you now.

Drowning in the depths of desire,
A prisoner to this burning need,
Yearning for a love untold,
Caught between longing and a fractured creed.

SILENCE BECOMES THE ECHO

Why do we fall for those who break us apart,
Who leaves jagged pieces scattered in our hearts?
How can I find the strength to move on,
When your ghost haunts me, lingering all night long?

How can I seek the peace of sleep,
When your shadow dances in the dreams I keep?
Once, it was magic— a refuge so sweet,
But now it's a prison, where my agony and longing meet.

I wake to a heart heavy with grief,
And a mind that finds no sweet relief.
The torment you've left behind is my only companion,
A constant ache, a never-ending expansion.

TORN BY SILENCE

H ere I lie, shrouded in shadows, deep,
Wrestling with choices I'm too weary to keep.
In the stillness, a quiet peace unfurls,
A bitter solace, where no sweet release swirls.

Let the smoke curl, slow in the air,
As these four walls silently stare—
A weight that presses against my soul,
Whispers creeping, claiming control.

How I long for someone to break these chains,
To lift me from this bed where torment remains.
Another wound, another scar laid bare,
A fractured mind, a storm I can't repair.

I carve the pain just to feel it bleed,
These thoughts—restless, yet hard to heed.
The rhythm of my heart—raw, unyielding—
Mirrors the hurt, the lies, the unhealing.

Every weight, every burden, every deceit,
I stir the chaos and embrace the heat.
I long for you to witness this slow descent,
As I unravel, piece by piece, in silent torment.

UNRAVELED IN STRENGTH

What do you do when everything you hold dear
Is hanging by a thread, trembling in fear?
What do you do when unseen hands tighten
Around your soul, with cruelty and spite in?

I am trapped, bound in a cage of despair,
A puppet, my strings pulled, gasping for air.
The weight of it all crushes, unyielding, unkind,
I am lost in the chaos that rages inside.

Emotions crash like waves, fierce and wild,
Yet I lock them away, like a grieving child.
I yearn to silence the beat of my heart,
To drown out the echoes, where sorrow starts.

How do I bear to see those I cherish,
Turn their backs, let the love we shared perish?
Why can't I find peace in being just "okay"?
Why do these shadows return every day?

But then, I remember—I am more than my pain,
I rise from the depths, from the blood and the rain.
I won't be confined to the darkness I fear,
For I've learned to embrace the light drawing near.

The weight may still press, but it no longer defines,
I stand stronger now, unbroken, unblind.
The tides of emotion no longer crash over me,
For I've learned to swim, to let my spirit be free.

I have tasted the depths, and now I will soar,
I reclaim my heart, and I ask for no more.
The shadows may linger, but they will not claim,
For from the ashes, I rise, untamed.

No longer a puppet, no longer restrained,
I stand with courage, no longer chained.
I embrace the fire, the fight, the flame,
For now, I'm a force, no longer the same.

And when the storm rages, I meet it with grace,
I am the tempest—no longer displaced.
I am the struggle, the fight, and the light,
I rise from the ashes, unbroken, in flight.

OLD FAMILIAR SONG

I search for brilliance in every soul I find,
Like seeking stars where the moon has left behind.
I know none are perfect—least of all, me—
I bear my flaws, yet still stand free.

My heart is a canvas, scarred and worn,
Each mark a battle, each wound reborn.
But deep inside, a flicker remains,
A light that pushes through unseen chains.

If I reach into the depths of your soul,
And touch the light that once made me whole,
Only to watch it dim and fade,
Know this: my love will never trade.

If your peace is born from causing pain,
Let it fall like rain, wash away the stain.
I've danced with hurt, embraced the cost,
Now it flows within me like an old familiar song, never lost.

Reflection Prompts

25. In The Cage of Thought

When you've felt trapped by your own thoughts, how did you find a way to break free and regain control over your emotions?

26. In the Quiet Between Dreams

What does the space between wakefulness and sleep reveal about your deeper desires and unresolved emotions?

27. Crown of Contradictions

How do you navigate the emotional contradictions of loving someone who both inspires passion and causes pain?

28. When Silence Becomes the Echo

How does silence affect your emotional state—does it offer comfort or amplify feelings of loneliness and isolation?

29. Torn by Silence

In moments of emotional turmoil, how do you balance the desire for connection with the temptation to withdraw into silence?

30. Unraveled in Strength

When overwhelmed by negative emotions, what gives you the strength to rise above despair and regain your sense of stability?

31. Old Familiar Song

How do your flaws shape your journey toward self-acceptance, and what have you learned about love and healing through your struggles?

CHAINS AND CHOICES

Exploring the tension between freedom and confinement, where love, fear, and self-imposed limits intersect and shape the choices we make.

This section delves into the complexities of personal liberation—both the chains that bind us and the choices that allow us to break free. Through these poems, you will confront the paradoxes of love, the struggle between remaining in the comfort of what is known and stepping into the unknown. As you navigate the questions that cage us and the decisions that define our paths, you will find that breaking free is not always a simple act, but a continuous journey of self-discovery and acceptance. Here, the exploration of love, isolation, and the power of choice opens up new possibilities for personal growth and transformation.

CAGED IN QUESTIONS

I feel too much, and then too little,
Caught in a cycle, sacrificial.
My emotions, wild, defy all sense—
Shifting, intense, without defense.

My mind, a storm that never rests,
Endlessly searching for the next test.
Will I pass? Or will I fall?
Is there redemption, or none at all?

Do I believe in something higher,
Or am I lost to doubt's fire?
My thoughts, a prisoner, locked away,
In a cage I can't escape today.

IS LOVE JUST A GAME?

I hate the doubt that clouds my mind,
Is this love, or just a thrill I can't unwind?
I give my soul, my time, my grace,
And still, I'm left with this hollow space.

Where is the love that burns so bright?
Where's the trust that wraps me tight?
Was it lost in the heat of our desire,
Or simply the cost of playing with fire?

A love unspoken, fierce, and raw,
A bond that tempts, that makes me withdraw.
I searched for it in whispered dreams,
But now I wonder if it's as it seems.

The pull is dangerous, the ache divine,
A hunger that leaves no room to define.
I reach through shadows, feeling for light,
Drawn to you, craving this endless night.

THE FINAL DANCE

Once, your laughter filled the air,
But now, my heart can no longer bear.
Again and again, I reached for you,
But now, our dance is done, the curtain's due.

I loved you with a flame that scorched my core,
Yet you let it fade, leaving me wanting more.
I yearned to drown in fury, to let rage unfold,
But in your shadow, I unearthed truths untold.

Through every tear and each bitter ache,
My love was never lost, nor could it break.
It was mine to hold, to honor and keep—
And I've paid the price, no matter how deep.

A GAME PLAYED

I was just;

A game you played,
A thrill you chased,
A drug you'd take,
A mark you'd make,
A face to seduce,
An ego boost,
An occupant of your time,
An adrenalizing crime.

BREAKING THE CHAINS

What's the cost of this twisted dance—
To burn in flames, then lose the chance?
To climb the heights, then crash and sink,
Chasing desire, only to blink?

When my tears are drained, my heart cracked wide,
My love lingers, but still I hide.
You carved your name into my veins,
Listened to my screams, then freed the chains.

But I won't remain in the shadows you cast,
Your grip weakens, slipping fast.
No longer yours, no longer bound—
I rise from darkness, without a sound.

THE LOVE I OWE

Is this love a labyrinth of dread and delight,
A silk-wrapped dagger that pierces the night?
Is it passion's torment or a siren's demand,
Pulling me deeper with its phantom hand?

The torment rises like a blackened tide,
Its whispers claw, leaving nowhere to hide.
Your shadow lingers, a specter on my chest,
Yet I crave your touch, though it tears at my rest.

A crimson thread binds me to this pain,
But deep within, a voice begins to wane—
"Shatter the mirrors that distort what you see,
For only in ruin can you set yourself free."

The chains of the past, cold as a grave,
Must break as the night consumes what it gave.
To heal is to bleed, to drown and arise,
Reborn in the ashes of love's cruel disguise.

When the darkness calls with its siren plea,
And the edge of despair feels too close to me,
I'll drink from the void, let its shadows consume,
Till I bloom anew in the midnight's gloom.

For to love in truth, one must first decay,
Shedding the lies that led them astray.
In the embers of ruin, I'll find my decree—
That only through darkness can the spirit break free.

THE PRICE OF SOLITUDE

When I seek inspiration,
I imagine my destination—
A place beyond this moment,
where my spirit finds elation.

I can't remain here much longer,
My heart whispers that something feels wrong,
and it's getting stronger.

I remind myself, that I am who I am,
And freedom comes at a price—a price I'll pay,
To break free from the worries that weigh me down,
To stop rushing through life, just to turn it all around.

Free from the poison in my mind,
Free from the masks that people hide behind.
It's time to slow down, to take it all in—
To look at where I am, and where I've been.

What have I truly achieved?
What lessons lie beneath the pain I've grieved?
I think of that little girl who once sat on a roof,
With her eyes to the sky, and her dreams as proof.

She would whisper to the stars,
Hoping they'd guide her through life's scars.
And now I know, it's time to believe—
That the power to change is mine to receive.

Reflection Prompts

32. Caged in Questions

How does uncertainty shape your decisions, and what steps can you take to find peace when you feel trapped by your own thoughts or emotions?

33. Is Love Just a Game?

How do you distinguish between love that is genuine and love that feels fleeting or uncertain, and what role does vulnerability play in your relationships?

34. The Final Dance

How have you found closure in a relationship or situation that has ended, and what lessons did you learn that shape your future connections?

35. A Game Played

Have you ever felt like a pawn in someone else's game, and how did that affect your sense of self-worth and autonomy?

36. Breaking the Chains

What was the turning point that allowed you to break free from something that held you back, and how did it feel to rise stronger after the struggle?

37. The Love I Owe

How does the process of facing your deepest truths and embracing self-acceptance lead to a transformation in how you experience love?

Reflection Prompts

38. The Price of Solitude

How does solitude help you gain clarity about your life and direction, and what are you willing to sacrifice to achieve the freedom you seek?

THE PATH OF POWER

Exploring the emergence of inner strength, the reclaiming of personal truth, and the transformative power of choice and self-awareness.

This section charts the journey toward empowerment—the process of recalibrating the self, confronting illusions, and embracing the truths that lead to personal freedom. Through these poems, you will encounter the shifting dynamics of love, belonging, and self-actualization. The path is not linear, but one marked by the tension between the mind's illusions and the quiet but undeniable force within that propels you toward authenticity and power. Here, the choice to awaken and align with your true strength is yours.

SYMPHONY OF BELONGING

Beyond the shadow of doubt, my mind is clear,
Every misstep, every "wrong turn," a path to here.
A truth once lost within the chaos now shines,
For every stumble was a step toward this divine design.

The voices that roared have softened to whispers,
Their discord now a melody of quiet wonder.
Can you hear it? The music is alive, breathtaking,
A rhythm that carries me, a song of awakening.

I dance unbound, laughter rising like a flame,
Singing my soul's song, unafraid, untamed.
Each breath pours into the melody's embrace,
A harmony of connection, a love I can trace.

Your heartbeat guides me, my rhythm entwined,
Each step we take feels written in time.
Isn't this wondrous, this dance we've found?
A perfect waltz, where destiny and joy abound.

RECALIBRATION OF SELF

It's time to reset my inner programming,
To elevate my mind to a higher plane,
Unlocking deeper truths of fear and perception,
And shifting my focus toward a grander direction.

Reassessing my goals, reaching for the stars,
Transcending old pain, leaving behind the scars.
No more frustration, no more hesitation—
I'm moving toward light, embracing harmonization.

THE RISE OF TRUTH

Those who hold power will start to break,
As we unravel the truth they've tried to fake.
This web of illusion, built on deceit,
Will crumble beneath the strength of our belief.

We must turn inward, where answers lie,
The truth concealed where our shadows hide.
It's time to rise, together we stand,
Rebuilding the self with our own hands.

THE TRUTH OF LOVE

Is love truly all we need,
A fragile hope, a whispered creed?
A bond so deep, it breaks the night,
Where one soul mends, and ends the fight.

Yet when I wake, and open my eyes,
I see the darkness, where hatred lies—
A curse that haunts, that never dies,
Passed down through time, beneath the skies.

But now, it's time to sever the thread,
To silence the voices, the words we've said.
It's time to rise, and light the gloom,
Let love reclaim what hatred consumed.

THE CHOICE IS YOURS

It's easy for your mind to fray,
To let the weight of doubt lead you astray.
It's easy to surrender to fear,
To close your heart and disappear.

It's easy to ignore what's true,
To let the darkness cloud your view.
It's easy to accept the silence,
And never question what it's costing you.

But it's hard to steady your own mind,
To rise above, to seek, to find.
It's hard to love when trust is torn,
To face the doubts that leave you worn.

It's hard to heal, to make amends,
To gather the strength to start again.
But the choice is yours, no need to choose,
Easy or hard, the path to lose.

You decide which way you'll go—
To let it break, or let it grow.

THE POWER WITHIN

I never knew the strength of my mind,
Until I learned the truth, so hard to find.
The mind, a tool both sharp and wise,
Yet often misused, beneath disguise.

This world is steeped in shadowed games,
Where truth is twisted, and nothing's the same.
So, whose side are you willing to choose?
Are you playing for the light, or destined to lose?

Will you awaken from the dream you've known,
Or remain in slumber, numb and alone?
For remember, nightmares are dreams too—
A reflection of the fear we let slip through.

Will you rise above the world's cruel abuse,
Or stay entranced, still bound by its use?

THE MIND'S ILLUSION

Our mind, a master of disguise,
Weaving illusions beneath our eyes.
But it's up to you to realize,
To see beyond the twisted lies.

Will you be ruled by doubt and rage,
Or rise above, free from the cage?
Can you step back and simply see,
The tangled web of your own mind's plea?

Not every thought is truth, my friend,
Some are just echoes that never end.
For once, step out of your view,
And try to walk in another's shoes.

Think for yourself,
break free from the spell,
Or risk the cost of mental hell.

The power's yours,
the choice is clear,
To untangle your mind,
or live in fear.

Reflection Prompts

39. Symphony of Belonging

How did you find a sense of belonging after a period of feeling disconnected, and how has chaos played a role in your personal growth?

40. Recalibration of Self

When have you outgrown a version of yourself or a part of your life, and what new values or goals have you embraced as part of this evolution?

41. The Rise of Truth

How has confronting difficult truths shaped your understanding of yourself, and what power lies in embracing what has been hidden?

42. The Truth of Love

How has love both healed and challenged you, and how can you cultivate a love that transcends hurt to foster growth?

Reflection Prompts

43. The Choice is Yours

Reflecting on a decision that required you to face something difficult, what did you learn about yourself through that choice, and how does it shape your future?

44. The Power Within

When you felt powerless, what internal resources helped you reclaim your strength, and how can you reconnect with that power during self-doubt?

45. The Mind's Illusion

What patterns or beliefs shape your perception of reality, and how can you begin to challenge the mental "cages" that limit your potential?

REFLECTIONS AT THE CROSSROADS

Confronting the pivotal moments where choices shape our destiny, where we must face the cost of transformation, and where the stories we tell ourselves are rewritten.

This section explores the critical junctures in life where we must reckon with the price of change, the tension between truth and illusion, and the power of reinvention. At the crossroads, we find ourselves at a moment of decision—where our past, present, and future intersect. The poems in this part reflect the inner conflicts and revelations that arise when we confront the need to reinvent ourselves, reclaim our truth, and dance with the strength required to walk a new path.

THE PRICE WE PAY

The world is fractured, hearts unspoken,
Behind our walls, we live half-broken.
Each soul carries wounds that never heal,
Fear of the past makes us afraid to feel.

Can we undo the scars we've earned,
Or is this pain the lesson learned?
We hide our hurt, we mask the shame,
But in the end, what do we gain?

You build your fortress, lock it tight,
But at what cost, when you lose the fight?
We're all just souls with shattered hearts,
Caught in the battle where healing starts.

We're all wounded, searching for grace,
But ego blinds us to each other's face.
Stop the blame, tear down the shame—
We're more alike than we are the same.

THE CROSSROADS WITHIN

As the road ahead begins to split,
I stand in thought, unsure of it.
Each decision echoes in my mind,
Each voice I hear, a sign to find.

Which path shall I walk, which way to go?
What's the cost, and what will I sow?
Will I rise or fall, soar or sink?
I pause, I breathe, and start to think.

Change, relentless, calls my name,
In forms both wild and unashamed.
I follow the signs, wherever they lead,
Through tangled roots or skies freed.

No matter the direction, I will stay true,
To the essence of who I am, through and through.

REINVENTING THE MIRROR

I struggle with identity
as if I'm begging for some trace of approval,
Chasing the echo of who I was,
yet the reflection feels so distant, so removed.

The person you once called me is now a stranger,
Her face was unfamiliar,
lost in the pages of this life's strange wager.

She played her part, shifting roles with ease,
The game was in the change, the thrill of the breeze.
But where does the mask end, and the true self begin?
Am I the one I sought, or just lost in a spin?

I'm crafting the me that I've longed to become—
Bold, unshakable, impossible to outrun.

Bound by the chains of perfection,
yet I've found a secret grace,
Falling in love with the flaws I once wished to erase.

They say, "Love yourself," but "Don't forget to care,"
"Give to others, but don't be consumed by the snare."
Is it a balancing act, or a silent mental hell?
Trying to please them, while your heart swells.

THE STORY I TELL

My mind is a labyrinth,
too many thoughts consuming my space,
Some of them aren't even mine,
but they still have a place.

I try to navigate them, one by one,
But losing myself in them?
It's a tempting escape.
The drama, the suspense, the dark allure,

What happens next?
Is she a lover, or something more obscure?
Movies unfold inside my head,
each scene a tangled thread—

I can't tell if I'm awake, or lost in some nightmare instead.
Am I captive to the chaos of my own mind?
Oh, what a lovely invisible crime.

Don't believe all I write, it's not always my fight—
Perhaps I'm recounting someone else's plight.
Or maybe, just maybe, these words hold my truth,
A reflection of the pain I've concealed since youth.

But in the end... are we not all the same?
Writers of our stories, bound by our names.
The words flow freely, like ink on the page,
But whose story am I telling, in this literary cage?
You're the reader, so tell me true—
What makes a good story, when it's told by me, or you?`

THE SECRET OF CREATION

Creation—
what a spark, a tingle in the veins,
A shiver of truth, amidst the world's pains.
Beneath the chaos, the hurt, and the scars,
Beauty flickers—hidden among the stars.

Without suffering, how do we know our worth?
Without the veil, how do we touch the Earth?
The lies we tell, the masks we wear,
They lead us nowhere, but still, we care.

The world's a stage, an illusion we follow,
We chase the light, but the shadows swallow.
Leaders speak of freedom, but it's a fleeting sound,
And we're all just waiting to be unwound.

Can we break free from the web we've spun?
See the threads, each choice undone?
Is this the truth we've feared to see—
A reflection of who we've come to be?

So yes, my words may seem a touch too bold,
But are we not tired of the lies we're told?
The truth is there, just out of reach,
Waiting for the mind, the heart to breach.

In the madness, there's a secret to find,
A freedom hidden deep in the mind.
The choice is yours, the path is clear—
To chase the truth, or stay in fear.

DANCE OF TRUTH AND STRENGTH

Why am I angry?
I was deceived, played for a fool,
Told to suppress, to follow the rules.

But the truth?
A shadow, twisted and thin,
A mask of comfort, hiding the sin.

They cast me down, a spark meant to fade,
Yet in silence, I found the strength I'd never trade.
The pain, the grief—they became my guides,
In their shadows, my true self hides.

I've learned to listen, to stand alone,
To uncover the strength that's always been my own.

Why am I at peace?
Because I've found my worth,
To embrace myself, to honor my rebirth.

In quiet moments, I've learned to see,
The strength within, where doubt used to be.
In the depths, I found clarity,
A truth that spoke in stillness, a sacred rarity.

Now, I rise—not with fury, but grace,
For in stillness, I've found my sacred place.
No longer bound by the past or the fight,
I stand tall, embracing my inner light.

Reflection Prompts

46. The Price We Pay

What is the cost of remaining closed off from others, and what might you lose by refusing vulnerability and connection?

47. The Crossroads Within

How do you make peace with uncertain decisions, and what is the most important thing for you to hold onto during moments of doubt?

48. Reinventing the Mirror

How do you navigate the balance between changing yourself and staying true to who you truly are?

49. The Story I Tell

What stories about your worth and capabilities have been shaped by external influences, and how might rewriting them shift the direction of your life?

50. The Secret of Creation

How can you bring about real change and growth without tearing things down, and where in your life can you tap into your creativity to make a positive impact?

51. The Dance of Truth and Strength

How has adversity revealed your inner strength, and what truths about yourself have emerged through your most challenging experiences?

THE JOURNEY OF BECOMING

Embracing the continuous evolution of the self, where transformation unfolds, and the rewriting of one's story becomes the key to unlocking new possibilities.

In this section, the poems explore the transformative power of self-awareness, the ongoing battle between old beliefs and new truths, and the cycles that propel us toward growth. The journey of becoming is not linear, but marked by moments of rebirth, revolution, and redemption. As you navigate through the fog of uncertainty, you are reminded that you hold the pen to your own narrative—each choice, each shift in perspective, leading you closer to the truth of who you are meant to be.

REBIRTH

My mind drifts when darkness calls,
Confronting the fear of inevitable falls.
I've seen the truth of my fragile breath,
But it's not the final word on death.

I am light, I am love, a truth I'll find,
Though doubts and fears are sometimes blind.
I fear losing my home, my place,
Where love and trust can fill the space.

But the burden inside does not own me,
I choose who I am and what I'll be.
I fight the dark thoughts that reside and confine,
And rise with strength, realigning my mind.

I write to release the weight I bear,
To let go of pain and breathe the air.
I love my life, my soul, my tribe,
And in my heart, my truth resides.

I chose this path to face my fears,
To shed the past and dry my tears.
The old me fades, the new me heals,
And now, reborn, my spirit feels free.

REVOLUTION OF THE MIND

Let the rules crumble, let them fall,
Who are they to dictate, to stand so tall?
We'll shape our own path, untamed, unknown,
Rewriting the script with hearts of stone.

They told us to fit in, to play their game,
But their boundaries are empty, no one to blame.
We'll rise from the wreckage, let them see,
In the ruins of their order, we set ourselves free.

REWRITING THE NARRATIVE

C hallenge the mind, question what they've sold,
Unlearn the lies they've forced to mold.
Tear down the walls of their deceit,
And free your soul from their concrete.

Vision sharper, see beyond their veil,
A new truth rises, no longer frail.
Build from the cracks, where the light breaks through,
Where hearts unite, yet remain true.

Forge your path where no one's led,
In the spaces between, we rise instead.
No chains to bind, no rules to keep,
Only the power of the truth we seek.

But even in freedom, paradox remains—
The rules that bind us, still play their games.
To break them, we must first know their weight,
To free ourselves, we must challenge fate.

For in our defiance, the rules take shape,
A structure we must bend, not break.
In rejecting the system, we find a new form,
Where the power lies not in rebellion, but in reform.

THE BATTLE OF BELIEFS

ace the mirror, confront what you fear,
Dive deep into shadows, where truth disappears.
Right feels like wrong, and wrong whispers sweet,
In the silence of doubts where darkness meets.

Live in the storm, love in the fire,
Burn with a passion that takes you higher.
A right can sedate, but wrong holds you tight,
And in the grip of its power, you lose the fight.

Heart against mind, a war without end,
Where beliefs twist and bend, and none will mend.
Truth is a phantom, a whisper, a lie,
A haunting refrain, that you can't deny.

CYCLES OF BECOMING

Death and rebirth, the soul's quiet waltz,
In every ending, we find the spark that haunts.
The more you search, the deeper the abyss,
For in every question lies a dangerous bliss.

Each answer born, another riddle hides,
The more you know, the less you confide.
And with each step, the mind expands,
But knowledge slips like grains of sand.

In the silence of truth, we are undone,
For in seeking the light, we become the one
Who fades into the dark, chasing what's lost—
In this dance of becoming, we pay the cost.

IN THE FOG OF REDEMPTION

Thirsting for redemption,
I wander endless spirals,
Craving salvation,
lost in the mist of shattered trials.

Is there a hand to grasp me from the void,
Or must I plummet deeper, where sanity is destroyed?
The whispers of my soul tremble in the night,
A prayer swallowed whole by the consuming fright.

Where is the light that once burned within?
Has it faded, or have I forsaken it in sin?

THE EDITOR OF YOUR FATE

In a world of shadows, where truths are denied,
Faces wear masks, and secrets collide.
You move through the noise, caught in the blur,
Where the lines between real and false often stir.

Be true to your heart, but don't fear the strain,
For growth isn't gentle—it thrives in the pain.
You're both your own hero and the villain you fight,
Trapped in a cycle, but still, you take flight.

The doubt you carry isn't just in your mind,
It seeps into your bones, through spaces you can't find.
But it's your inner light that refuses to dim,
A fragile flicker, but steady within.

You're the author, the one who writes the tale,
But also the editor, trimming what's frail.
Each mistake you make leaves scars on your skin,
Reminders that growth is a battle within.

The pen in your hand, it's not just for show,
It's the power to change what you think you know.
With every misstep, with every slip,
You're rewriting your story, finding your grip.

The road is real, full of cracks and doubt,
But it's yours to walk, and there's no turning out.
You may stumble, you may fall, but still, you rise—
You're the master of your fate, no need for disguise.

WHISPERS ON THE WIND

Tell me,
Did you hear the whispers, the breath of the wind?
It was the trees that spoke, their roots deep within,

I saw her—wild, untamed,
A grin that sparked the night, unchained.
She moved, a flame that twisted and danced,
Unshackled joy, in its purest trance.

Above her, the sky was dark, alive—
A flock of birds, like shadows, they dive,
Their song—a cry from the earth to the sky,
A truth that trembles in the quiet night.

Then from the mountain, a cry so loud,
It cracked the silence, pierced the shroud.
The shadows stretched from the forest deep,
And in their grasp, she began to weep.

But still, she rose, fierce, untold,
A hunger for the light, relentless and bold.
In the darkest depths, she felt it near—
A flame within, burning through her fear.

She shouted to the world, no softness in her tone,
"Through the fall, we rise, unbroken, alone.
The dark will shape you, the shadows will teach,
In the depths of despair, our souls can reach."

RAW AND UNMASKED

She writes with ink that stains her soul,
Words that pierce, words that console.
Her laughter echoes, soft yet deep,
A rhythm born from secrets she keeps.

She moves like fire, untamed and wild,
A force that speaks, though soft, beguiled.
A voice that howls through moonlit skies,
A melody that never dies.

She is the storm, the calm, the fight,
A flickering flame in the endless night.
Her beauty lingers, sharp and sweet,
A force of nature none can defeat.

She feels the weight of every scar,
Yet in her heart, she's come this far.
From shadows dark, she takes her stand,
A fierce and steady, trembling hand.

For she is power, raw and real,
The fire's burn, the truth we feel.
She knows the cost, the path she's paid,
Yet still, her soul will never fade.

She is me, unmasked, unbowed,
A woman fierce, a spirit proud.
Stripped bare, yet unapologetic,
Alive and whole, raw and poetic.

Reflection Prompts

52. *Rebirth*

What part of your old self has been hardest to release, and how can embracing the new version of yourself lead to greater freedom and strength?

53. *Revolution of the Mind*

How has a shift in your thinking or emotions transformed the way you approach life, and what new possibilities have emerged from that change?

54. *Rewriting the Narrative*

What story have you been telling yourself about your life, and how could changing that story help you make choices that truly reflect what you want and need?

55. *The Battle of Beliefs*

When have you been torn between conflicting beliefs or values, and what did you learn about your true self in navigating that inner conflict?

56. *Cycles of Becoming*

What recurring patterns have you noticed in your growth, and how can you use the lessons from past cycles to guide your future evolution?

57. *In the Fog of Redemption*

When have you felt lost or uncertain, and what actions helped you find clarity or redemption during that time?

Reflection Prompts

58. The Editor of Your Fate

How can you take ownership of the key moments in your life and edit your story to reflect the person you are becoming, rather than just who you've been?

59. Whispers on the Wind

How has a moment of connection to something greater than yourself shifted your perspective on your life and purpose?

60. Raw and Unmasked

When have you dared to show your true self, and how did that experience change your understanding of your heart's desires and the strength of your authenticity?

JOURNAL PROMPTS FOR INTROSPECTION

1. **Transformation:**

   - What has been the most significant transformation in my life so far?

   - How did I feel before and after this transformation?

   - What steps or changes did I make to embrace this transformation?

2. **Self-discovery:**

   - What have I recently learned about myself that surprised me?

   - How do I define who I truly am, and how has that understanding evolved?

   - What aspects of myself am I still discovering or unsure about?

3. **Healing:**

   - In what areas of my life do I still feel the need for healing?

   - What are the steps I can take toward emotional or physical healing now?

   - How do I know when I have truly healed from a past hurt or experience?

JOURNAL PROMPTS FOR INTROSPECTION

4. **Resilience**:

   - When have I shown resilience in the face of adversity?

   - How do I stay strong when life becomes challenging or overwhelming?

   - What personal qualities do I possess that help me bounce back from difficult times?

5. **Introspection**:

   - What thoughts or feelings have I been avoiding, and why?

   - How often do I engage in self-reflection, and how does it affect my well-being?

   - In what areas of my life do I need to dig deeper to understand myself better?

6. **Empowerment**:

   - What actions or beliefs make me feel empowered in my life?

   - How can I take more ownership of my decisions and choices moving forward?

   - When do I feel most confident and in control of my destiny?

JOURNAL PROMPTS FOR INTROSPECTION

7. **Spirituality**:

   - What role does spirituality play in my life, and how has it shaped who I am today?

   - How do I connect to something greater than myself, whether that's nature, faith, or community?

   - What practices or rituals help me feel spiritually nourished and at peace?

A Note of Gratitude

To the Reader,

I want to take a moment to express my deepest gratitude to you for picking up this collection and allowing these words to resonate with you. Writing this book has been a journey of self-discovery and reflection, and it's an honor to share it with someone who is open to walking alongside these thoughts and emotions.

Each poem within these pages represents a small piece of a larger story—one of struggle, growth, vulnerability, and transformation. As you read, I hope you find echoes of your own journey within these verses, and that they offer you both comfort and challenge. The act of writing these poems was not just about creating art, but about finding connection through the unspoken and the unseen.

Thank you for opening your heart and mind to this work. Your time, your attention, and your willingness to engage with these words mean more to me than I can fully express.
It is my sincerest hope that this book has given you something to reflect upon, something to feel, and perhaps even something to hold onto as you continue along your own path.

With gratitude,
Monica Yarbrough

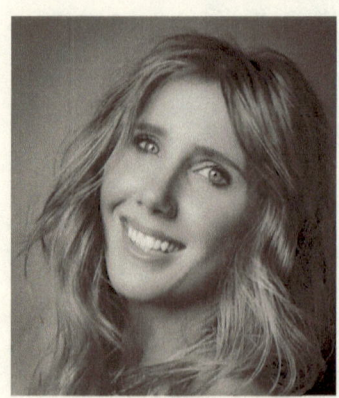

@Houston.mgallery

About the Author

Monica is a poet, writer, and seeker of truth whose work explores the intricate layers of the human experience. Her poetry ventures into the spaces where words dissolve into silence, where light and shadow converge, and where chaos meets clarity. With vivid imagery and raw emotion, she invites readers to journey inward, urging them to confront the unspoken truths that lie hidden in the quietest corners of the soul.

In The Silence Between Words, Monica captures the profound stillness that holds our deepest wisdom, delving into themes of identity, love, inner conflict, and self-reflection. Drawing from both personal experience and a deep, intuitive connection to the world around her, her writing is an authentic invitation to explore the path of transformation and renewal.

When she's not writing, Monica finds renewal in nature, drawing peace and inspiration from the world around her. Whether horseback riding, relaxing outdoors with her dogs, or wandering nature's trails, she connects deeply with the natural world. Her bond with horses teaches her patience and the language of intuition, while time spent with her dogs fills her with joy, grounding her in life's simplest, most profound moments. The laughter and love she shares with family and friends nurture her spirit, reminding her of the deep connections that sustain her.

Monica is deeply committed to understanding the complexities of the human mind and the forces that shape behavior. Her curiosity fuels a lifelong pursuit of knowledge, blending insights from philosophy, psychology, and personal experience. Through her writing, creative endeavors, and ongoing exploration of the human condition, she seeks to connect mind, heart, and spirit, embracing both the challenges and joys of her journey toward personal growth and understanding.

www.ingramcontent.com/pod-product-compliance
Lightning Source LLC
Chambersburg PA
CBHW020756130626
46554CB00006B/2213